`5/11`

A FIRST
LOOK
AT
REPTILES

Angela Royston
Photographs by Oxford Scientific Films
Illustrated by Adrian Lascom
Belitha Press

The publishers wish to thank the following for permission to reproduce copyright material:

Oxford Scientific Films and individual copyright holders on the following pages: Anthony Bannister 15 top; Eyal Bartov 5 right; G I Bernard 16 top; Waina Cheng 6 top; Peter Cook; J A L Cooke 25 centre, 26/27; Treat Davidson/Photo Researchers Inc 25 bottom; Stephen Downer 22; Carol Farneti/Partridge Films Ltd 20; Michael Fogden 21 centre, 23 bottom; W Gregory Brown/Animals Animals 6 bottom; Mark Hamblin 12 top; Mark Jones 4 bottom; Pam Kemp cover; Michael Leach 15 bottom, 18 bottom; Zig Leszczynski/ Animals Animals 5 left, 7 top, 9 top and bottom, 19, 25 top, 27 bottom right; Tom McHugh/Photo Researchers Inc 28/29; S Nagaraj 4 top; Stan Osolinski 8, 12 bottom, 27 top; Richard Packwood contents page; Avril Ramage 11 top; J H Robinson/Animals Animals 21 top; Peter Ryley 14; Jany Sauvanet/Photo Researchers Inc title page; Maurice Tibbles 24; K G Vock/Okapia 16 bottom; Kim Westerskov 7 bottom; Belinda Wright 21 bottom, 23 top; Len Zell 26 inset.

First published in Great Britain in 1997 by
Belitha Press Limited,
London House, Great Eastern Wharf,
Parkgate Road, London SW11 4NQ

Text copyright © Angela Royston 1997
Photographs copyright © Oxford Scientific Films and individual copyright holders 1993
Format and illustrations © Belitha Press Ltd 1997

Printed in Portugal

ISBN 1 85561 742 0

British Library Cataloguing in Publication Data
CIP data for this book is available from the British Library

Editor: Veronica Ross
Designers: Frances McKay and James Lawrence
Consultant: Steve Pollock

Words in **bold** are in the glossary on page 30.

Title page picture:
An emerald tree boa from South America.

Contents page picture:
An agama lizard.

Contents

What is a reptile?

The animals on these pages are different shapes and sizes, but they are all reptiles. They have many things in common, such as a dry, scaly skin.

▲ This is a mugger crocodile. It waits for an animal to come by, then grabs it with its huge jaws.

▼ Tortoises have a hard shell to protect them. This giant tortoise is from the Galapagos Islands in the Pacific Ocean.

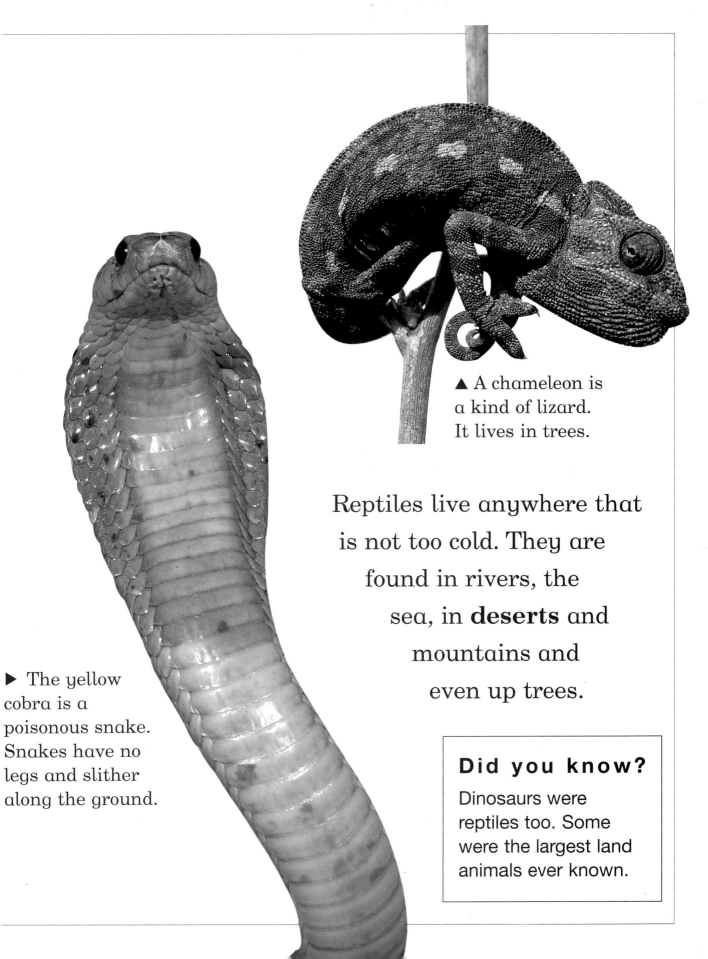

▲ A chameleon is a kind of lizard. It lives in trees.

Reptiles live anywhere that is not too cold. They are found in rivers, the sea, in **deserts** and mountains and even up trees.

▶ The yellow cobra is a poisonous snake. Snakes have no legs and slither along the ground.

Did you know?

Dinosaurs were reptiles too. Some were the largest land animals ever known.

Types of reptile

There are four main groups of reptiles. Tortoises and turtles have a **shell** on their backs and four legs. Snakes and lizards have long bodies and skin covered with **scales**. Some have forked tongues.

▼ Turtles look like tortoises but they live in water. This turtle lives in the sea.

◄ This boa has the remains of legs. They look like white claws.

Crocodiles and alligators have strong tails and big jaws with pointed teeth. The fourth kind of reptile is the tuatara.

▼ The tuatara has spines along its back. It lives in New Zealand.

▲ A gavial is a kind of crocodile. It has a long, thin snout.

Body heat

Our bodies make heat from the food we eat, but reptiles can't do this. Instead a reptile takes its warmth from its surroundings.

When a reptile needs to warm up, it moves to a warm place. It may sit and **bask** in the sun. When it is warm enough, it moves into the shade.

◀ This desert iguana has a white skin. White **reflects** the sun's heat and keeps the iguana cool.

When a reptile is too cold or too hot, its body does not work properly and it moves about very slowly. Reptiles that live in hot places rest in the shade during the day or **burrow** underground to stay cool.

◀ An alligator warming up in the sun.

▲ When a crocodile gets too hot, it opens its mouth to cool off.

Reptile skin

Many people think that snakes are slimy but, like all reptiles, their skin is hard and dry. Many reptiles are covered with horny, waterproof scales, made of **keratin**.

Tortoises and turtles are protected by a hard, bony shell. Only their head and legs stick out. When it is in danger, a tortoise pulls its head and legs into its shell.

▲ Crocodiles have thick, horny skin.

▶ A turtle's shell is made of bone. Over the bone is a layer of skin covered by thick, horny scales.

Did you know?

Lizards do not shed their skin all at once, like snakes do. Instead large flakes of old skin fall away, like flakes of dandruff.

▼ A snake sheds its skin from time to time. Under the old skin is a new skin.

Teeth and jaws

Most reptiles cannot chew their food. Instead they swallow it whole. A snake can swallow an animal larger than its head.

▼ A crocodile's teeth and jaws.

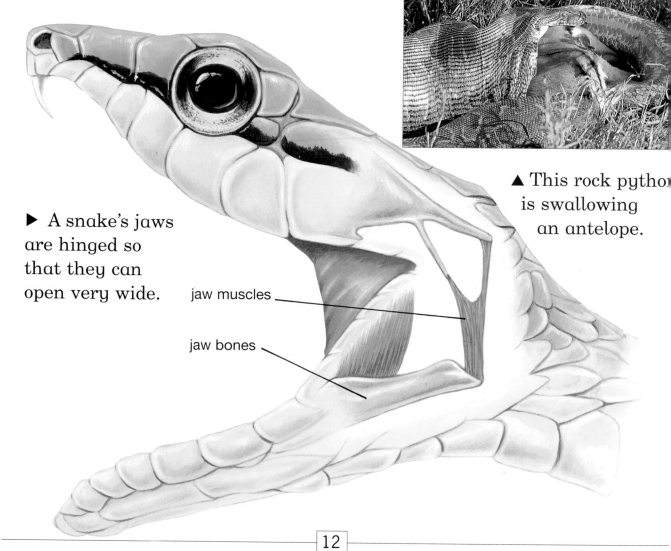

▶ A snake's jaws are hinged so that they can open very wide.

jaw muscles

jaw bones

▲ This rock python is swallowing an antelope.

Crocodiles use their sharp, pointed teeth and long jaws to snatch and hold their **prey**.

Lizards that eat plants have blunt teeth that are set in their mouths like the edge of a saw.

Turtles and tortoises have no teeth. Their mouth is a hard, horny **beak** instead.

▲ A lizard that eats leaves.

▶ Most lizards have sharp, pointed teeth for grabbing insects.

Moving around

The way a reptile moves depends on its shape. Tortoises walk slowly, lizards run, snakes slither and turtles swim. Turtles use their **flippers** like oars to pull themselves through the water.

A crocodile swims by moving its huge tail from side to side. A crocodile can move fast over the ground even though it only has short legs.

A snake slithers by pushing parts of its body against the ground and moving the rest of its body forwards.

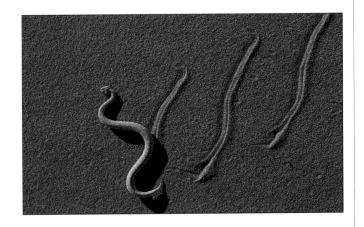

▲ Snakes that live in the desert cannot slither through hot sand. They swing sideways instead.

◀ Tortoises plod along very slowly. Their heavy shells keep them safe from attack.

▼ This flying gecko cannot really fly. It stretches out its legs and glides from tree to tree to escape danger.

Eyes and ears

Crocodiles and alligators have eyes on top of their heads. They lie quite still with only their eyes above water, waiting for prey. Crocodiles have an extra see-through eyelid on each eye. They close this eyelid when they are underwater to protect their eyes.

Snakes cannot shut their eyes because they do not have eyelids. Snakes' eyes are covered with see-through scales.

▲ A crocodile can see under water.

▼ A snake's eyes are always open.

Did you know?

Scientists think snakes could give us an early warning of **earthquakes**, because they can feel tiny movements in the ground.

Most reptiles have **eardrums** hidden under the skin. Snakes don't have eardrums, so they can't hear sounds in the air. But they know when another animal is close because they feel the **vibrations** in the ground.

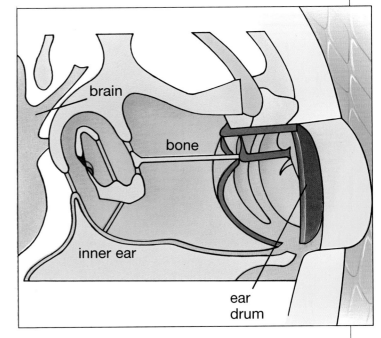

▲ The inside of a lizard's ear. The eardrum picks up sounds through the skin.

▶ A tuatara has a third eye on top of its head. This eye can see light but not shapes.

Smell and taste

A reptile's senses of smell and taste are almost the same. Snakes and lizards 'taste' the air with their tongue. The tongue takes the taste to smell **detectors** in the roof of the mouth. When snakes or lizards smell something interesting, their tongues flick in and out very fast.

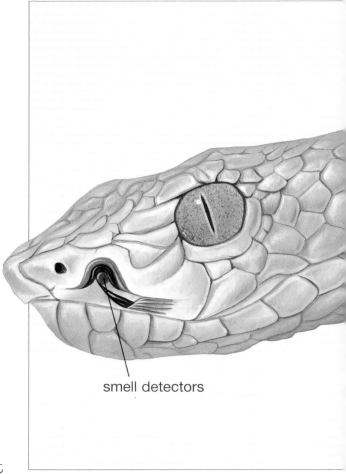

smell detectors

▼ A chameleon catching an insect with its tongue. If it tastes nasty, the chameleon will spit it out.

▲ Snakes and lizards have smell detectors in their mouths.

Most animals use sight, sound and smell to find food. But some snakes also have heat detectors in their skins, which can pick up the heat from an animal's body.

▼ A pit viper tastes the air with its tongue. It also has heat detectors on the front of its head.

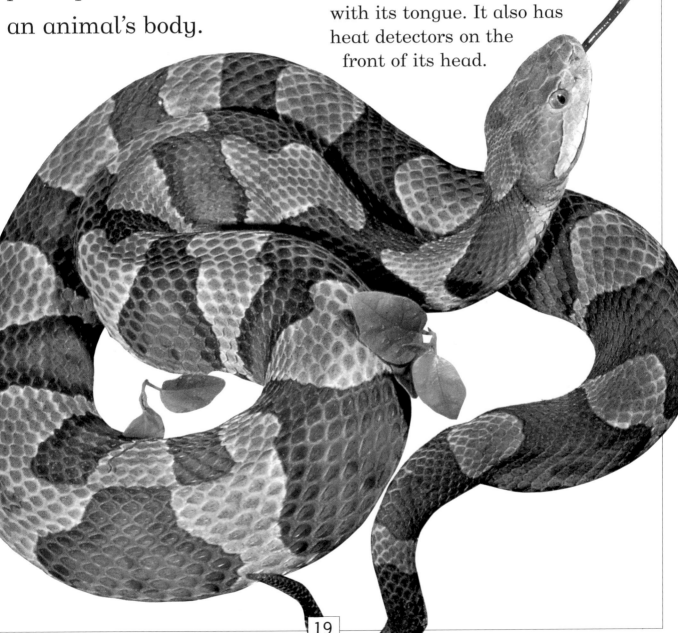

Defences

Some lizards and snakes are hard to see because they blend in with their surroundings. This helps to protect them from other animals. Crocodiles and alligators are so big, no animal would dare attack them.

Some poisonous snakes are brightly coloured and animals learn to avoid them. Some harmless snakes copy their colours. This makes other animals think they are poisonous too.

▼ A chameleon changes from green to brown or yellow to match the colour of its surroundings.

Did you know?

Some lizards can break off their own tails. The lizard escapes, leaving its attacker with the tail.

▲ The snake at the top is harmless, but the one below it is poisonous. Their enemies can't tell them apart and leave them both alone.

◀ When a frilled lizard is attacked, it hisses and opens a large frill of skin to make itself look bigger and fiercer.

Feeding

Most lizards feed on insects. Chameleons catch insects with their long, sticky tongues. Some lizards eat larger animals, while others feed on plants. Tortoises eat mainly plants, but they sometimes eat insects.

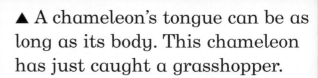

▲ A chameleon's tongue can be as long as its body. This chameleon has just caught a grasshopper.

◀ This Australian saltwater crocodile has just caught a fish between its huge jaws.

Crocodiles and alligators eat frogs and fish. They also lie in wait in the water for other prey. When an animal stops to drink, the crocodile grabs it and holds it under the water until it drowns.

All snakes feed on other animals. Some have **fangs** that inject poison into their prey to kill them. Other snakes coil around their prey. They squeeze their victim tightly until it stops breathing.

◀ Egg-eater snakes can swallow eggs that are wider than they are.

Eggs

Most female reptiles lay their eggs on land, often in a hole in the ground like a nest. Even turtles and crocodiles that live in water come ashore to lay their eggs.

▲ Sea turtles crawl up the beach to lay their eggs in the sand. The turtles then return to the sea.

Some snakes and lizards keep their eggs safe inside their bodies. The mother gives birth to live young.

◄ These two young snakes are hatching out of their eggs. Snakes' eggs have a leathery skin, not a hard shell like birds' eggs.

► This turtle's egg has been cut open to show the tiny turtle growing inside.

A reptile's egg lets in air and has a **yolk** inside which feeds the young. When the young reptile is ready to **hatch**, it tears a small hole in the shell with a special egg tooth.

► American alligators bury their eggs in a nest of rotting plants. The heat from the rotting plants keeps the eggs warm.

Looking after young

Most reptiles do not look after their eggs or young. Turtles and tortoises cover their eggs and then forget them. Many eggs, and some young reptiles, are eaten by other animals.

Some kinds of snake look after their eggs, but not their young. Pythons and cobras coil around their eggs to keep them warm. Some lizards guard their eggs from attack.

▼ These young turtles have just hatched out of their eggs.

▼ Newly-hatched turtles scurry as fast as they can to the sea.

▶ A young alligator clings for safety to its mother's tail.

Crocodiles are the best reptile parents. The female watches over her young for several weeks after they have hatched.

▶ This diamondback rattlesnake has just given birth to young.

World of reptiles

There are over 6000 different kinds of reptile. They live in most parts of the world, except in very cold places.

Millions of years ago, dinosaurs and other kinds of reptiles lived on Earth and then died out.

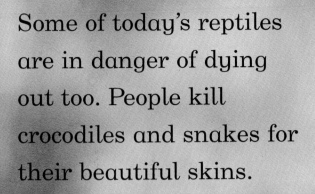

Some of today's reptiles are in danger of dying out too. People kill crocodiles and snakes for their beautiful skins.

But the biggest threat is the destruction of the reptiles' **habitat**. There are now laws to protect these amazing animals.

▼ The komodo dragon is the largest lizard alive today.

Glossary

Bask To lie in the warmth of the sunshine.

Beak A hard part of the mouth. Tortoises have a beak, like a bird's beak, instead of teeth.

Burrow To dig a tunnel or hole in the ground for shelter.

Desert Land which has little or no rain. Deserts are often very hot.

Detector Something that senses the presence of something else.

Eardrum A thin layer of skin inside the ear. Sound waves make the eardrum vibrate. The vibrations are passed through the ear to the brain which hears them as sound.

Earthquake A violent shaking of part of the Earth's surface which may split open.

Fangs Sharp, pointed teeth.

Flipper A flat, broad limb that some animals have to help them move through water.

Habitat The natural home of any plant or animal.

Hatch To break out of an egg.

Keratin A hard substance from which horns, nails, claws and reptiles' scales are made.

Prey An animal which is hunted for food by another animal.

Reflect When light or heat is turned back by a surface.

Scales Small, flat plates that cover the skin and protect it. Fish scales are made of bone, but reptile scales are made of keratin.

Shell A hard covering that protects from harm. Tortoises and turtles have shells made of bone.

Vibrations Very fast backwards and forwards movements.

Yolk The yellow part of an egg. The yolk is a store of food that feeds the young animal while it is growing in the egg.

Key facts

Largest reptile Saltwater crocodiles can grow more than 7 metres long – that is longer than two family cars parked end to end.

Heaviest reptile The leatherback turtle is the heaviest reptile. It can weigh as much as 725 kilogrammes – heavier than three Sumo wrestlers.

Smallest reptile The dwarf gecko is only 34 millimetres long from the end of its nose to the tip of its tail. This is about the length of your little finger.

Longest reptile The reticulated python from Southeast Asia grows up to 10 metres long.

Longest poisonous snake The king cobra, which lives in India and Southeast Asia, grows up to 4.5 metres long. It is probably the most dangerous snake in the world, although its poison is not the most deadly.

Most poisonous snake A sea snake's poison is 100 times more deadly than any other snake's.

Largest meal A python 5.5 metres long was found with a leopard in its stomach. Another had swallowed a whole bear.

Most caring mother The Nile crocodile carries her young in her mouth until they are big enough to look after themselves.

Largest lizard The komodo dragon is 3 metres long. It eats small deer and pigs.

Fastest lizard The Strand racerunner can run at up to 28 kilometres an hour over short distances.

Longest living reptile Tortoises live longer than all other animals. The oldest known tortoise was 152 years old when it died.

First reptiles The earliest reptiles lived 340 million years ago. They were about 20 centimetres long.

Largest dinosaur Brachiosaurus grew more than 24 metres long and weighed 50 tonnes. Its head towered 12 metres above the ground.

Index